Other Words For Grief

poems by

Lisa Marie Rollins

Finishing Line Press
Georgetown, Kentucky

Other Words For Grief

ACKNOWLEDGMENTS

Thank you to *As/Us Literary Journal* for their publication of "There is No
Statue Here" and "I Fail to Read My Ancestral Chart."

Thank you to San Francisco Foundation for awarding this manuscript, under
another title, The Mary Tanunbaum Award. Thank you to Finishing Line
Press for giving this book a go.

Thank you to all of my writing and creative communities VONA, Callaloo,
JTHAR, Crowded Fire Theater Company and BRAVA Theater for the
Women for their deep respect and sustained support of me and my work.

Gratitude to my manuscript readers and dear friends Vickie Vertiz, Joseph
Rios, and Jordan Gonzales for their invaluable feedback and love during this
process.

Thank you to my intimate loving friends - you know who you are - who have
sat next to me and lived with me in the darkness deep after my mother's
death.

Thank you to my family.

Publisher: Leah Maines
Editor: Christen Kincaid
Author Photo: Nathan Yungerberg
Cover Art and Design: Bread Slice Design, Oakland, CA

Table of Contents

"The condition of Black life is one of mourning."

~A mother of a black child, as spoken to writer Claudia Rankine, author of CITIZEN.

Other Words for Worth

value, n.   1. [estimated worth or importance; valuation.]
Syn. goodness, merit; see quality, *see **deserving.***

deserving, mod.   1. [to have a claim to]
Syn. be worthy of, have the right, to be suitable for.

*see **wanted.***

Black Pearl

I know it's dangerous. The sea gods could notice me throwing this wish back in to the ocean. There it will float alongside horses, starfish and mermaids. Yet perhaps they won't see and the maids will catch and place it inside an oyster so the gods cannot spot it. Perhaps my wish will settle inside the meatflesh of the shell with all that sand, salt and turn blacker as years pass and it is forgotten. Perhaps a fisherman will find it, chip his tooth as he chews the meat and pass it on to his cherished wife. There she will be with my wish clasped about her neck black as the inside of its previous shell closed tight at the bottom of the sea. Perhaps the gods will not notice my forgotten wish; perhaps they will return it because it is not coming true for me, but instead for the fisherman's wife. can see it now, outside her door a lover stands, sand on his shoes and seaweed in his pockets. He is knocking, knocking while inside she is filled with fear that tides and swells, seawater on a full moon.

Into the Wreck

after Adrienne Rich

the ocean has no memory my brother says. *that's not true* I counter
the ocean is filled with bones of slaves, pirates and mariners

it remembers well and longer than we will ever live
cleanses itself even as it holds tight to carcass, wreckage, blood.

what was formed when god fashioned us binds together with pebbles
chips of starfish, seaweed and burnished mythical ships

I am asked to dive into this wreck and sew myself back together
I will with or without you, and all my hope is inside this pearl

only when we both breathe deep
point our fingers into the "v" to shave open the waves

dive down, down to remember, into spoils together,
only when we both claim its treasure its baubles its barnacles

let our lungs fill with water   let us drown   let me drown
swallow this shackle of history and float again to the surface.

Postcard Song #9

Dear Lisa

    I have heard tell of Aran and Angalo the two giants that spit and made our Ilocano bodies on the coast in the north land. It is rumored (or historical truth?) if you look at the north star hard enough on any winter solstice night in these islands, Angalo, one of the giants who made this earth, will appear in the sky. You can see stripes where he spits out and the liquid from his mouth falls to the ground, there, where the stars shoot across the sky in deep black. If you walk that way, then follow his sword it will aim you due north to the highest hill at the edge of Luzon. Once you reach that point, your body will be filled with starlight and you can walk across the sea.

Postcard #10

Dear Lolo,

    I wonder where my brown body begins and where it ends and if that ending is blackness and which side belongs to either, if any. What fantastical conversations we would have had. The ones we have now with your photo on my altar, greet me each morning, an oceania salutation with flame. Both me and my sister wander Luzon's fuzzy coast in our dreams mixing sand and fish bones. I used to think it was an auntie singing to me behind the trees but now I know it was you. Rollin dice, counting quarters until you can bet a dollar and singing black girl blues songs in Spanish, long before you imagined an apóng babae like me.

Diaspora

[reincarnation]

our bodies held in bandage configuration
arms swaddled next to our chests

crib bars puncture through
flimsy veils of white protection

no one says slavery out loud
yet over and over our blood is shed

what gets sacrificed
our childhood   our bodies   our belonging

this time around is a subtle torture
more than a drip of water on my forehead
less than whipping on my back.

There Is No Statue Here

~ for those children taken from Haiti after the 2010 earthquake

for the wealth of bodies moved across ocean and land
unaccompanied wrapped for presentation at the airline gate

for the girl who opens her hands, wilted grass clutched for hours of flight
grass falls as her new mother scoops her into crisp Christian arms

for the safety in white spotless sheets and freshly pressed skirts
sharp pencils and a grand piano sticky from her syrup fingers

microglass of memory the moon shines through
thin steel slats of the shade over her new bed

2 years gone   she doesn't sleep yet
in the dark she remembers her sisters, o the smell of cooking legim

whispers words to herself like
kontan, papa, soulye, mande Bondye padon and *don't forget.*

Spell to Find my \/ father
(birth)

It's a myth midnight is the witching hour. Light the first candle when dawn breaks as magic is strongest when earth is still cool with dew.

Gather bits of hardened clay you found in your mom's garden. Position them below the altar around the streaked redgray chalk drawing gifted from the stranger who recreated your face at the coffee shop.

Rest 1 white candle at the top. Add the piece of baby hair your mom hid inside the photo album when she sent you to college. Fold in the photo of you in foster care one month infant body laying in a crib you do not recognize.

Call up the day you spoke to the man who could be your uncle and he hung up on you. Mix firmly with ghost voices who speak Spanish in your dreams, your love of fish and poki, your desire for a brown baby boy. Ball these up and light them on fire. Let the ashes drip down atop the chalk picture. Whisper his imagined name to the smoke. Blow hard into the mirror. Wait.

The Porch

Holly Park Projects, Seattle Washington

I heard a rumor you might be a Price. you heard 'bout them Price's yeah? That old man used to run those projects, sittin up on the porch with a rifle cross his legs and a handgun hidden at his hip, like this was the South. This ain't the South! Them young girls, they was always hangin round, pretty one's too, sniffing around him and his dope money like he was Jesus himself come to town to save em from sleepin in corners or up in some flea bag motel. You sure you don't got some of that Price blood in you? Yeah, I can see it. That nose and them cheeks an' you looking all pretty and light like your daddy. Where you get them oriental eyes girl? Your momma must been one of them girls, hangin round outside that porch. That old man always did like them pretty girls, man, he shore did.

I Fail to Read My Ancestral Chart*
47.4831° N, 122.2158° W

How do stars position if you do not know the exact time of your birth? Small notations line blank segments of this hospital documentation, almost illegible. They indicate how long her labor difficulty yet not the time it ends when I entered the world. So to examine points of stars where my moon sits locations of planets could require the sum of multiple angles. There is mathematics involved here numbers sperm egg and flash of spirit a cocktail of wondering. The astrologer wrinkles her nose. She has heard this story repeatedly. She sighs and reaches for my palm instead runs her fingers over the lines as if they are the only thing concrete As she squints I know what can be read can't be simply a shroud of silence because my hand is here my thighs and belly thickening with age and my birthfather dying without seeing my face. And from stories I hear, without wanting to.

Other Words for Grief

longing, n.   1. [strong, persistent need or craving]
Syn. yearning, pining; *see **desire**.*

desire, v.   1. [to wish for]
Syn. long for, crave, covet; *see **want**.*

      *see **hunger**.*

"Portrait of a Woman Fallen From Grace into the Hands of Evil."
after Carrie Mae Weems in London

I am a fallen woman, I admit it
legs open to receive you I laugh   you pierce
me on the bed where you lay with your wife
curse into your mouth   sully my name

when golden dawn light rides the blinds
I gather my stray Underground fare ticket
you finger my curls, swell with demand
kiss me again

face down, the pillows smell of her
stray blond hair tangles into my black curls
I carry her until I bathe off the stink of you
comb through my locks and soap the sweat gone

my breasts covered with your bite marks
fading, fading fast.

Ways of Reading

Sherrie isn't as smart as she thinks she is you murmur
stretching across the car seat to finger my seatbelt
unbuckle it then reach up to turn my chin
its fun right? right in front of her?
I vomit and bend to the rubber floor mat of your BMW
smelling men's cologne and the coke binge
we had for three days last week

fuck! you scream a cut across your wrist
I can't see any blood but my eyes are red red
wishing there was romance left in my hands
you push me out the black car door
wishing on the gravel under my feet
wishing out to the strawberry field on my right
I bend again   *I'm sorry.*

Cancer

my mother is dying and I still sneak out of the house
meet strangers in the woods behind the hick bar
let them touch me so I can just feel

it's a shallow drop off where my ankle hits the creek
moonlight drips grey over the water flowing downhill
miniature falls splash droplets into my whiskey

his joint ember lights his dark eyes
guides my steps across, wearing her thick garden boots
no bra and a raw sheep's wool sweater

he fingers my red belt buckle, lips on my neck
I watch the moon, still holding my glass
as I hear her ring the nighttime dinner bell.

Postcard #17

Dear Adam

Today is her birthday. We are sitting around the table,
no one will make mention this might be our last July
together. Uncle Paul is cracking jokes with my brother.
Some tall tales about women and cheap beer and the
wet flats of the Aberdeen Bay. My brother tries to top
his story, calls up my grandfather, our family gas
station and something about fireworks. My mother and
I lock eyes. She is having a good day, hasn't called out
to the Lord once while holding the black bucket that
runs red when her insides come out. Today the blue of
her eyes is clear and mischievous and it reminds me
of the day I caught her flirting with my ex boyfriend,
patting his knee and whispering a dirty joke in his ear.

Fall in Rochester, WA

mom squats over the last of the season
green pea rows and warns me she is feeling rebellious
the surgeons orders frustrate her
they just want to make money
her uterus and the tumor both belong to her
she's had it for 73 years *why let it go now?*

she talks about the tumor like it is a child in her belly
the tumor wants cake, on tuesday it wanted cookies
I gave it apples instead, granny smiths from the tree by the barn
those are the best because of how the sun hits them
I squat to rest my arm around her

I don't know how to give her women earth rituals
or prayer song ceremonies for womb releasing
God is gonna take this tumor out of my body
I'll be cancer free by Christmas, you'll see

we separate peas from shells
stroll back from the fields
her head on my shoulder.

Postcard #2

Dear Lisa

Your mother and I send greetings from Israel again. We've stopped at the same hot springs, so she can pick up the sea salts she so loves. There's been multiple fabric stores some with appointment, some without. Your mother's face is a concentrated woman bartering. The men in the shops stop for a moment when she begins to haggle, so like their wives, except she is a foreigner. They still try to take her money so when she feigns walking away they call her back. She has gotten the prices she wants three times. The fourth, she bought some fabric for you and didn't argue, not at all.

"Who claims this child?"*
for James Cagney, poet.

Come on home my dad says. He says it as if I am still 15 having run away again. As if coming home will make everything right. As if I am able to conjure my 12 year old self who believes skin to bone in his God the father. Maybe if I pray hard enough I will forget I am alien inside my own church walls or that I see cracks in the sanctity of these prayers. Maybe I will forget the mink oil smell of the pews, the stale taste of the bread of life and the wintry eyes of the assistant pastor when he sees my brown knees kneel in supplication.

Nest

I am jealous of who will love you when you are old. She will bring you tea while you write. I will be nothing but gold fieldgrass or perhaps a bluebird on your window, reading over your shoulder. I will note what woman's leg you want to touch, how many times you have re-read Montoya and if as a old man you still find his vision of the fields sharp. I will resist pecking her eyes out or instead perhaps I will be her companion, fly to her kitchen door, eat crumbs she leaves me after she has made your dinner. I will eat them, eat them and think of days when we would kiss and kiss and kiss with too much whiskey in our veins.

Passover

After Toi Derricotte, Empress.

between my fallopian tubes and uterus
there is a block in passage

flash of spirit misses its mark
flesh red and tissue pink stillness

bottle tree captures my son or daughter
refracted before they can pass

ferryman sits greedy in wait
for coins placed over my eyes

offering of lamb and smoke
yet blood paints this entry again

a night spent in prayer, a meditation mat
another instant for death to reverse itself.

Psalm

When we first met I pulled from my deck over and over terrified and desperate to find you in it. Some days you are a preacher. Not the kind you confess to but they do anyhow. I do. You don't ask me for secrets yet they run out drip down cover me in blood only you seem to pardon. I pull the desert card and on the side of the road there is reddust and wind, sunfire making the prayer hold strong like Jesus whipping a prostitute so she can heal from pain anew. She kneels, is forgiven and stands looks at us standing across the highway, nodding because she can read what is between us. I can't translate. I shuffle again. I see a cavern and a waterfall. A Bear and Fish together and one does not eat the other simply lumber and swim side by side. I squint to read them. The very last pull for you it was pouring rain, my bedroom ceiling light leaking molded drops directly on to my bed cover. Magician slides by Fool and my hands wrinkle. The Fool walks off the cliff ready to dive without fear. This world is so cold, even small bits of love we accept we dine we devour. I ache and remember *love as thou wilt.*

Other Words for Bend

bow, v. 1. [twist, warp, curve, detour, turn;]
      *see **diverge**. see **deviate***

      *see **buckle**. see **collapse**. see **break**.*

Black Jack

you slip slaves into dark, wet chambers
steal them yourself, them stow away

bend bodies to fit clothing trunks
tucked inside white women's silk slips

locked until no one is looking
unlocked to vomit and spit on deck.

Jack, if true north is not due north how then do
you measure birth to death on your own black body?

The deck hand paints the name of the ship head
careful like a spell surrounding the bow

if even one syllable off it will turn
sour, the sea gods will notice and hamper

island to island communication
perhaps start a war from the confusion

browned maps blur not only with one another
damp with where they begin or end, and latitude

confuses with longitude and you pray
there is more than one way home, you pray there

is more than one home as this ship swallows
your hands it carries more than bodies

there are so many you cannot save
you touch fingers of the shackled black faces

that look like you in the mirror
you return below and weep yourself to sleep

you bow in honor as they exit the ship
turn your back, hoist the sail collecting more

salt on your cheeks
secrets in your stores.

To The Japanese Man at the Bar Who Asked Me if I Knew Filipinos Are the Niggers of Asia

So what you sayin
I'm a nigger nigger?

The Cross

I know you remember sitting atop the hill together when I showed you the blue bruises Elijah gave me when we came out of the dungeon. I knelt willing arms tied high, no bra. How well I took the flog and released. Bruises disappear but I am purged and hot all at once deep in caverns of this dark ritual. Deep inside desperation of his hands, of his blackness tied with his own death making me weep making him weep with all our curved sin. These days blood is everywhere. Across my sheets or dripping on the bath room floor down to my toes. These days death surrounds us. It is more than vocal ancestors we chant up for protection right now, more than bodies wrapped around bullets on these sidewalks. They strip us down naked, tie us up and whip us so we don't forget our place

July 2016. Why I don't Give a Shit if the Black Man Hanging from the Tree in Piedmont Park, Atlanta Was a Suicide or Not.

His head is the death bound despair of the enslaved. Arms hips legs a carcass walk with no spirit. Capable of being shot over and over, he drops again and again from the branch. They say he climbed on top a green trash bin to shimmy up the tree. They say there was a rope. What I know is that two men were shot down the day before his body appeared in the park. What I know is black bodies are dropping like crickets after the crop duster flies overhead. Mist wraps our little shells so we disappear from the land quiet. What if his body was already coated in blood from watching reels and reels and miles and miles of footage of black bodies falling. What if like a slave mother slicing the neck of her newborn or drowning her in the river holding the swaddled body close, he crouches in the stream shoulder-deep in grief. What if he simply wanted to drop, join the pain overtaking him before he exploded. What if instead of receiving bullets he snapped himself with the satisfaction of escape, crossing rivers, crossing wide wide grassland leaving us with a freedom map, greased and woven to perfection in his braids.

Black Ophelia

I.
thing about fish people we don't need air
you think your chokehold silences us?
you think underwater we don't know how to breathe?

II.

a rusted red wheelbarrow sits waters edge
a truck backs up tires slick from rushed roads
holds as three bodies roll from its bed

land and sound out as a low hallowed bell
in the steel bowl, the wheelbarrow edge tips
heaven cries on this holy dumping ground

wet with mud, blood and fear they sink down slurp
ankles wound together with rope and bricks
how many eyes watch guard under algae

low down where you exile our black flesh fresh
veins swell as the blood rots months sealed airtight
waterlogged eyes fill with seeping swamp mud

you want us to burst and die here again
until disintegrated flesh cant speak
be sure your sins will find you out

III.

I make offering to the maid and crone
who guard these waters. I hear they sleep deep
wake cold feed off dying fish and damp moss

If offering please them they claw their way
past cypress root past tadpole past lilypad
to count the bodies brought to these back woods

corpse arms cross-tied sunk to the swamp bottom
the maid swims down to kiss the blue dead lips
breathes mermaid cousin magic to closed lungs.

I call too these ancestors you murdered
the swamp maid sings, the crone combs her wet hair
slaughtered bodies quell and mud overturns

Hidden beneath the reeds we will watch you
shine your gun sharpen your knife rip mouth gags
always at war to take your country back

you will feel our eyes on your bare white neck
will not notice the crones hair in the reeds
as it winds up into silent rushes

under your boat the swamp floor darkness grows
littered with the slain, dust to dust to mud to water
it is a most fertile place to set root

the feet of our dead will touch the bottom
settle sprout link fingers with others tossed
shoot to the sky, cypress wings swim upward.

we'll set lookouts count wheelbarrows count bodies.
It has always been a holy war here
fight for the souls of the living and dead

dance after church in cemetery dark
whiskey and finger beats glass bottle trees
cinnamon spit chewed with ginger root bite

suck hard and spit
this land has been in holy war
so all we need do now is raise the dead.

UNTITLED

youtellmeloveisboundlessbutalliseearethelimitsofwhitelove
whereitstopswhereitcanthearyoutellmeloveisboundlessbut
youstilldontcareaboutourpainyoustillletusdieyoustillwatch
ussufferyousaythatloveisallthingsbutyourealiaryourealiar
therearelimitstoyourwhitelove

IknowthelimitsofwhiteloveIcantellyouwhatterrorisandyou
sayforgiveforgivewearestillbeatenIwanttobelieveintheplace
whereloveneverendsbuticountonalltenfingersdeadbodies
becauseoftomanyhandsandmomImsorryImsorryitsounds
likeImsayingyoudontlovememomImsorrymomIfeelyour
boundlesslovenowthatyouaredeadyouknowhowtoprotect
meIknowyousurroundme

whitelovehaslimitseventhoughyouredeadthewhitegirlsat
schoolflickinglitcigarettebuttsatmybrownskinherboyfriend
askswhyI'mstillaviginshecallsmeniggerhepushesmeagainst
thewallspitonmesaysmyblackskinissuglywhilehefondlesme
momIknowyoudidntknowwhenyouwerebehindyour
bedroomdoorpraying

Iknowthelimitsofwhitelovethecopssaytheyknowbestrestrain
hertothegroundshesawildanimaltothemkneeinherfaceshes
nakedmomImananimaltothemtootherearelimitstoloving
animalsbecauseonedayyoumighthavesplitthierskinoper
breakthemopenyoumighthavetocontainthemyoumighthave
toeatthemalive.

Bad Girl

after Jamaica Kincaid's "Girl" and Michael Jackson's "Bad"

step up when spoken to. look that man on the street hollerin at you in the eye, spit on him if necessary. this is how you elbow a man who tries to touch you wrong. when you are in danger this is how to break a man's nose. you are not scared of bugs or animals, you definitely do not run squealing away from nature. you open your eyes, close your mouth, watch and listen. you can hear the voices of the gods and goddesses in the forest, near the sea, or walking the red desert. you respect life. you have compassion. this is how to love your sisters. this is how to make your home a safe space for them to breathe. this is how you breathe. this is how you find time to breathe. this is how you plant lavender and squash. this is how to fertilize them. this is how you change a tire, this is how you call a cab, this is how you take the bus. this is how you can tell what game is. this is how to run your own game. this is how to use a knife. how to chop wood. this is how to start a fire. how to keep warm. this is how to run from trouble. this is how you run toward joy. sit with your legs wide so you can ground with the earth. stand with your legs wide so you have balance then you won't get pushed over. this is how you call impossible ideas into being. this is how you light candle spells. this is how you be. this is how you recognize love. this is how you know when to fall all in to love. this is how you know to fall all in. this is how. you are loved. this is how you love.

NOTES / WORKS CITED

Epigraph
> from New York Times article, "The Condition of Black Life is One of Mourning". 2015, by Claudia Rankine.

from **Palm**
> "Love as thou wilt" is a quote from one of my favorite guilty pleasure, non- magical fantasy series *Kushiel's Dart* by Jaqueline Carey.

from **Black Jack**
> after viewing a National Park Service photo of the crew of the *Rathdown* in 1892 near San Francisco. In the photo there are 20 men, at least 12 are African American, 10 of which are identified as non enslaved Black Mariners.

from **I Fail to Read my Ancestral Chart**
> title is a line from "Economic Miracles" in Sun Yung Shin's book of poems, "Skirt Full of Black".

from **"Who claims this child?"***
> for James who told me, *just write the damn thing* when I complained I didn't want my entire book to be about adoption. *who cares if it is the adoption manuscript? Write it, get it over with because sometimes the thing just has to be the thing, otherwise it is going to be the thing, over and over until you are done with it.*

Lisa Marie Rollins is a poet, playwright and freelance theatre director. She has been a writing fellow with *San Francisco Writers Grotto, CALLALOO London, VONA, Just Theater Play Lab, Joshua Tree Highlands Artist* Residency and will be a resident with *Djerassi* in late 2018. Her writing is published in *Other Tongues: Mixed-Race Women Speak Out, River, Blood, Corn Literary Journal, Line/Break, As/Us Literary Journal, The Pacific Review* and others. Lisa Marie wrote and performed her acclaimed solo play, *Ungrateful Daughter: One Black Girl's Story of Being Adopted by a White Family...That Aren't Celebrities* in festivals, universities and academic conferences across the US. She is currently developing her new play "TOKEN" which recently celebrated a staged reading with Crowded Fire Theater's MatchBox series. She is a *Directors Lab West* member and a Directing Fellow in the *Sundance Institute Theatre Lab*. Lisa Marie is a Resident Artist with Crowded Fire Theater and Artist-in-Residence at BRAVA Theater for Women in San Francisco. lisamarierollins.wordpress.com

CPSIA information can be obtained
at www.ICGtesting.com
Printed in the USA
BVHW04s1119180818
524549BV00005B/35/P